THE LIZARD SCIENTISTS

STUDYING EVOLUTION IN ACTION

Text by Dorothy Hinshaw Patent

Photographs by Nate Dappen and Neil Losin

Clarion Books
An Imprint of HarperCollinsPublishers

Clarion Books is an imprint of HarperCollins Publishers.

The Lizard Scientists

ISBN 978-0-35-838140-2

Typography by Carolyn Bull
22 23 24 25 26 RTLO 10 9 8 7 6 5 4 3 2 1

First Edition

PROLOGUE

I've always been fascinated by wild animals. Not birds—too easy to see—but creatures I had to hunt for, like finding buried treasure. One day when I was twelve or thirteen, exploring near my California home, I spied a lizard perched on a rock. Specks of bright blue gleamed in the sunshine, decorating his back. Luckily, the lizard was so wrapped up doing quick push-ups with his skinny front legs and spreading out his bright blue throat that he didn't notice me crouching a few feet away. He was too busy telling other lizards "This is *my* rock. If you're another male, stay away. But if you're

This is a fence lizard similar to the one I watched display when I was a girl.

a female, I'd like to be friends." I was immersed in the world of this intriguing animal, watching his private life unfold in front of me, a gift he didn't know he was giving. From then on, I was hooked on lizards.

My love of wildlife led to a Ph.D. degree in zoology and a career as an author, sharing great wildlife stories with young readers. So when a film, *Laws of the Lizard*, came to the 2017 International Wildlife Film Festival in my hometown of Missoula, Montana, I could hardly wait to see it!

As I watched, an astonishing variety of lizards captivated me as they flashed across the screen.

A hefty bright green canopy dweller slowly explores among the leaves.

A medium-size brown fellow perched motionless, head—down, on a tree trunk, springs out to snatch an unsuspecting insect from the ground, then zips back up to eat its prey.

Meanwhile, balancing on a slender twig, a tiny grayish stubby-legged lizard creeps ever so slowly along in search of a meal.

In the bushes below, a long-tailed cousin with bright racing stripes on its sides zooms away from the camera.

I knew I had to share the stories of these varied lizards that belong to just one scientific family—the anoles (Anolidae). Scientists use them to study basic principles of evolution and ecology in real time. I contacted the filmmakers Neil Losin and Nate Dappen, who had traveled around the Caribbean and Central America photographing these appealing lizards to show how they illustrate important processes in biology. They jumped on board to help me bring these lizards to life for you.

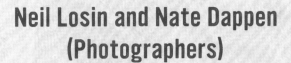

Neil Losin and Nate Dappen (Photographers)

Neil and Nate are a rare team—two Ph.D. biologists who love to pair science with adventure by sharing their knowledge and experiences through videos and photos. They met while studying anoles for their Ph.D.

Nate Dappen (left) and Neil Losin get a close look at an unusual anole.

research. Now their company, Day's Edge Productions, creates a variety of wildlife and nature films. In addition to their award-winning **Laws of the Lizard,** *they've produced* **The Lizard's Tale,** *a series of seven short videos exploring what anoles are teaching scientists about evolution and ecology.*

The team spans the North American continent, with Nate and his family living in the San Diego region of

California, while Neil and his family reside in the Miami, Florida, area. Neil and Nate travel frequently while documenting the wild world.

Neil (foreground) and Nate on the job.

CHAPTER ONE
STUDYING EVOLUTION OVER TIME

Fast-forward from the Wildlife Film Festival to October 13, 2019. I'd flown across the country from a land of brown grass and autumn leaves to a world of bright greens accented by brilliant tropical flowers in purple, gold, and orange and visited by iridescent blue butterflies and an abundance of lizards.

A female agama lizard perched on a post as if to greet my arrival at Fairchild Tropical Botanic Garden in Coral Gables, Florida.

"Why are you here?" this female agama lizard seems to be saying.

RIGHT: A male brown anole spreads out his dewlap.

The Fairchild Tropical Botanic Garden

The Fairchild Garden also has collections of plants that live in different environments, such as these from deserts.

Fairchild is a beautifully landscaped eighty-three-acre garden, home to more than 3,400 plant species from tropical regions around the world. Trails for visitors run through the area, circling several small lakes, including Center Lake, home of Dr. James Stroud's anole research site. In addition to the grounds being open to visitors, Fairchild sponsors such educational programs as Lizards on the Loose (see chapter 4), in which students in Miami area schools search for and photograph lizards so that scientists can keep track of where lizards are making their homes. Fairchild also provides laboratory space for student projects and for scientists like James.

The Fairchild Garden is known for its collection of beautiful orchids like this one.

As I walked through the garden gate, an aptly named male rainbow agama that looked like an artist's creation—bright orange head, rich blue body, and tail banded with gray, orange, and blue—showed up by the path.

Male rainbow agamas are hard to miss, with their lovely bright colors. Agamas are in a different family than anoles—lots of different lizards make their homes in the Fairchild Garden.

More lizards skittered about among the plants, moving so fast I couldn't see them. But from the rustling of the vegetation as they sped along, I knew they were there. This lizard lover's heaven was the perfect spot to meet with the ecologist Dr. James Stroud. The possibility of hurricanes and complicated travel made it challenging for me to encounter anoles in their home island environments, but anoles native to the Caribbean have moved to the United States mainland, joining the native green anole. James studies how these species share and divide the habitat in the Fairchild Garden over time.

As we strolled to his research site, James described the background for his work. Summarizing the major message of *Laws of the Lizard*, he said, "We've learned that anoles have independently evolved in the same set of different habitats on the four islands of the Greater Antilles—Puerto Rico, Hispaniola (which comprises the Dominican Republic and Haiti), Jamaica, and Cuba. On each island, one species specializes in living on the ground, another high up in the trees, one uniquely adapted to creeping along on twigs, and so on. It's a perfect example of Charles Darwin's principle of natural selection.

"Now I'm studying how four species that came to Florida from those islands and our native green anole are dividing up similar habitat at my site here in the garden. I've been checking on them twice a year since October 2015, longer and in more detail than most similar studies have attempted before." Long-term studies like this are rarely possible, making James's research important for understanding ecological relationships over time.

The bands of color in rock formations, like these in Canyonlands National Park in Utah, are formed by mineral deposits over millions of years.

The History of Change

Before the development of modern scientific thinking, people in the Christian world were taught that God had created each and every species and that these species stayed the same as when they were created. During the nineteenth century, when science developed as a form of inquiry that involved asking questions about the world rather than relying on religion for answers, ideas began to change. Charles Lyell and other geologists realized that the earth had been around for at least hundreds of millions of years, not just the six thousand or so years calculated from the Bible. And they were learning that the earth's geological makeup had changed greatly over time. Some scientists began to wonder: If the earth itself had been around so long and changed so much, what about the life that inhabited it? Had life changed as well?

Fossil findings, especially dramatic ones like those of dinosaurs, completely defied the concept of God creating a finite set of species that never changed. But if life did change over time, how did it happen? The biologist Charles Darwin made this question his life's work. In his landmark 1859 book, On the Origin of Species, he put forth a powerful explanation of how species change over time. He called it "the principle of natural selection."

The photographer Julia Cameron took this portrait of Charles Darwin in 1868.

Darwin's great insight was that inherited traits that help an organism live long enough to reproduce would be passed on through time. Traits that created a survival disadvantage would eventually disappear. For example, if a lizard can run fast enough to avoid being eaten by a predator, it has a chance of living long enough to pass on to the next generation the traits that go into its

speediness. Another lizard in the same environment might lack that quickness and become a predator's meal before it could reproduce.

Darwin's thinking about evolution was long-term—the concept that gradual changes would eventually lead to new species. New adaptations to the environment occurred over geological time, he believed. Now, thanks to studies of how animals with short generation times, such as anoles, adapt to changing conditions, we can actually study evolution as it occurs, even from just one generation to the next.

James Stroud shows me the characteristics of an anole.

Along the path, James noticed a lizard perched on a nearby railing. He quickly plucked it off to show me up close what makes anoles different from other lizards. He held the lizard gently in one hand by a front leg. "This guy is a male crested anole. See the loose skin under his chin? That's his dewlap. He can unfold it to show off to other anoles.

"Each species has its own dewlap color pattern, so they can recognize one another easily. They use their dewlaps to claim their territory—it's a way of saying 'this is my home.'

"Now look at his feet. See the wide part on the toes? These are called toepads. They allow him to move around easily—climbing tree trunks and clinging to them for long periods of time without difficulty and moving across smooth, slippery leaves without slipping off and falling. They are a major reason for the success of these lizards.

This green gecko has very obvious toepads but no dewlap.

This male crested anole has spread out his dewlap in order to be noticed.

"By the way, anoles are the only lizards that have both dewlaps and toepads. And they're all in the same scientific genus, *Anolis*, which is often abbreviated as just '*A.*'"

Iguanas have dewlaps, but they lack toepads.

How do toepads do their job?

Toepads are still a bit of a mystery to scientists. They are made up of expanded scales covered with millions of microscopic hairlike structures that help the toes cling to most surfaces so the lizard can easily climb trees and steep slopes, even if the surfaces are smooth.

Both anoles and geckos are champion climbers, thanks to their toepads. Scientists used to think the pads might produce suction that sticks the toes to a surface or that friction makes their feet stick. It turns out that neither of these mechanisms seems to do the job. It's more likely that tiny molecular forces are at work. Scientists keep studying this natural mystery to tease out the details of how they perform their vital function.

This brown anole watches the ground below for prey.

The toepads of the native green anole, which spends lots of time aboveground, are quite large.

The toepads of the green anole help it cling to glass and climb.

The Cuban crown-giant anole has big toepads that help it move around on slippery leaves near the tops of trees without slipping and falling.

James let the lizard go, and we continued strolling along. I looked around and noticed more anoles perched head-down on tree trunks in plain sight.

"Some of those are crested anoles, like the one I showed you," James said. "They're native to Puerto Rico. They look very similar to brown anoles, which are also here, but they came from Cuba. We call them both 'trunk-ground' species because they hunt by perching head-down on a tree trunk, waiting for prey to come by, then leaping down to the ground and grabbing it to eat."

We looked up to see a much larger, bright green fellow close to the top of a palm on the trunk. "That's a crown-giant that's native to Cuba," James said. "They spend most of the time in the crown near the top of the tree. We've found out that they have a varied diet, including other anoles and fruit. When we planted some seeds we found in their poop, the seeds actually grew. Before that, we didn't know that these lizards ate fruit."

We passed by James's lab building and walked until we left the path for his study site. As we crossed the treeless area with its short, mowed grass, James explained, "The populations I study live on this island. It's a peninsula sur-rounded mostly by water, but it's an island as far as the anoles are concerned. They don't like to cross open spaces like this—it's too dangerous for them. Small lizards are sometimes called 'nature's lunch box' because they are just the right size to be prey for larger animals."

As James pointed out the different types of habitats on the island, I could see just what I'd viewed in *Laws of the Lizard*—if your home is a tree trunk, it helps to be brown, so you're hard for a predator to see.

But at a top of a tree, among the leaves, green makes you less visible. The trunks are rough and fairly easy to cling to with small toepads. The leaves are smooth, so bigger toepads help to prevent lizards living in the canopy from slipping and falling. In this way, different species can share the same home, such as a tree, by living in different parts of it. They don't compete for space or food. Each kind occupies a different ecological niche.

I thought about the scientists who had come before, studying the anoles on the Greater Antilles and realizing that natural selection had acted over time on each island to produce species suited to different niches. Now scientists like James are building on their work and learning more about how these species are still changing and adapting as they encounter new environments and new challenges.

The knight anole from Cuba is a crown-giant, staying mostly high up in the tree.

CHAPTER TWO
INTRODUCING THE ANOLES

Anoles thrive in the Neotropics, the southerly parts of the Americas where it rarely, if ever, freezes. More than a hundred species live in the Caribbean islands and The Bahamas alone. Hundreds more inhabit Mexico, Central America, and South America. Some anoles skitter about on forest floors. Others hang out at the very tops of trees, rarely coming down to earth. And many species live in between. At least one streamside species in Costa Rica can dive into the water to escape predators, holding its breath for at least ten minutes below the surface.

A canopy-living crown giant anole shows his dewlap.

RIGHT: Some anoles perch on tree trunks waiting for prey.

Wherever they live, the diet of anoles is varied—basically insects, spiders, and even lizards smaller than themselves. Trunk-ground species may hunt on the ground as well as wait for prey.

Crested anoles sometimes hunt on the ground instead of waiting on a tree trunk for prey to come by.

This crested anole has caught an ant for dinner.

This trunk-crown anole from Hispaniola is licking nectar from the flowers of the tree. If it saw an ant or other insect come by, that could be dinner as well.

Some anoles that spend most of their time in the trees also lick nectar from flowers or even eat fruit.

Anoles are commonly brown or green, and they may be able to change color to match a background or to indicate a state of being such as fear or courtship.

This twig anole from Hispaniola matches the color pattern of the twig it perches on.

The trunk-crown anole from Jamaica is generally green.

It can also turn brown . . .

. . . or it can show a shaded variety of colors when in both light and shade.

Others have camouflaging color patterns.

Our native green anole (*A. carolinensis*) is just one of many species that can be green and, like many other anoles, can change color depending on the situation.

The native green anole can easily fool you by becoming completely brown.

This ability led to its other common name: the American chameleon. The true Old World chameleons, however, are not closely related to *A. carolinensis* and look very different.

This Old World chameleon is not closely related to anoles.

Several species of anoles from Caribbean islands arrived in southern states one way or another and have established themselves over time. They are believed to have arrived by accident in the wake of storms, in fruit shipments, or as escaped pets. Some, such as the brown anole from the Caribbean and the native green anole, also inhabit Hawaii and warm parts of California.

Lizards and salamanders

You've almost certainly seen lizards in your neighborhood or in a zoo setting such as a reptile house. Some people get lizards and salamanders confused, as they have the same basic body form, with four legs, a head, a body, and a tail. Lizards are reptiles, and like their snake relatives, they have scales covering their bodies that help hold in moisture so they can survive in dry environments. Most of them lay eggs that have shells and then hatch into tiny copies of their parents. Some give birth instead. Lizards are very adaptable, with thousands of species living in different environments in various parts of the world.

lizard

salamander

Salamanders may look like lizards, but they have very different lifestyles. They are amphibians that commonly have smooth, moist skin. Most of them need damp habitats, and they lay their eggs in ponds and streams. Their young grow up in water and gradually grow legs so that they can move onto land when they mature.

LEARNING ABOUT ANOLES

The tremendous variety of anoles and their successful adaptations to their specific habitats make them intriguing subjects of study for evolutionary biologists. In the 1960s, the Harvard lizard scientist Dr. Ernest Williams became fascinated by the anoles on the Greater Antilles islands—Puerto Rico, Hispaniola, Jamaica, and Cuba—and studied them in detail.

He discovered that each island had a number of species, each with adaptations that seemed helpful for living in the

Cuba

Jamaica

specific habitats where the individual anoles were found. To make matters more interesting, Dr. Williams realized that each island had the *same set* of habitat specialists. He coined the term *ecomorph* to describe the collection of traits—such as long legs or short ones, big toepads or small ones—that corresponded to the different habitats on the islands.

Dr. Williams gave names to the ecomorphs based on their distinct collections of physical traits and where they tend to spend most of their time.

1. Grass-Bush Ecomorph: Some anoles live on the ground, dashing through the grass, chasing prey, and avoiding predators. These small, slender lizards are characterized by a very long tail, lengthy hind legs, short front legs, and a narrow head. Their toepads are not well developed. They are usually brown and yellow, often with a stripe along each side.

2. Trunk-Ground Ecomorph: Many medium-size brown or olive-colored anoles belong to the trunk-ground ecomorph. They perch quietly on tree trunks, head-down, a foot or two up from the ground, where they can keep an eye out for predators and food. They can leap down to grab prey on the ground or turn tail and skitter higher if a predator threatens. Trunk-ground anoles tend to be stocky and strong, with long hind legs and short front legs. Their toepads aren't well developed.

3. Trunk Ecomorph: These anoles hang out on the mid level of tree trunks. They rarely go down to the ground or out onto the tree limbs. Their small bodies tend to be flat, and their legs splay out to the sides. The toepads on their front legs are larger than those on their hind legs, and their tails are relatively short. Their usually grayish colors blend into tree trunks.

5. Crown-Giant Ecomorph: The largest anoles are the crown-giants that live in the treetops. They have rather big heads and short legs with large toepads. The largest anole is a crown-giant named the Cuban knight anole, which can reach a length of seventeen centimeters (almost seven inches), not including its long tail. Crown-giants are usually green but can also change color to brown. Although an anole's diet consists mostly of insects and spiders, crown-giants also eat fruit and small lizards and birds.

4. Trunk-Crown Ecomorph: Trunk-crown anoles wander about in the trees more than most anoles. They tend to live at about adult human eye level or higher, but they may climb out onto branches or all the way up to the treetops in their hunt for food or safety. Their slender bodies bear short front legs, and their snouts are relatively long. Well-developed toepads help them navigate smooth tree limbs and leaves. Their green colors help hide them, but they may also change to different shades of brown.

6. Twig Ecomorph: These small lizards look quite different from the other anole ecomorphs. They have slender bodies, pointed snouts, and very short legs. Their mottled gray color blends in well as they creep along on thin branches, hunting for food. They are so adept at camouflage that they weren't even discovered until the 1960s!

Each of the four islands in the Greater Antilles is home to an anole species fitting into each of four ecomorph categories—crown-giant, trunk-crown, trunk-ground, and twig. As for the other two categories, Cuba and Hispaniola lack trunk anoles, and Jamaica doesn't have a grass-bush species. The crown-giant from one island looks very much like the crown-giants from the other islands. Owing to the ecomorphs' physical similarities across the islands, even the researchers sometimes have trouble telling certain species apart. This seems to be especially true with the trunk-ground ecomorph. The brown anole (A. sagrei) from Cuba and The Bahamas and the Puerto Rican crested anole (*A. cristatellus*) can look almost identical, except that the males have different-colored dewlaps.

When James held each in front of me and asked if I could identify which was which, with no dewlap showing, I couldn't tell them apart, and I guessed wrong.

At first glance, *A. cybotes,* from Hispaniola, could also be mistaken for the brown anole or the Puerto Rican crested anole, except that its dewlap is pale yellow.

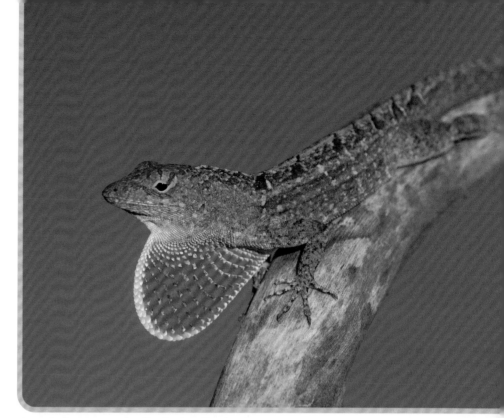

A male brown anole displaying its dewlap.

A. cybotes, a trunk-ground species from Hispaniola, can be recognized by its pale yellow dewlap.

A crested anole shows off his dewlap.

CHAPTER THREE
EVOLVING ECOMORPHS

Dr. Jonathan Losos

Jonathan Losos got his start in herpetology—the study of reptiles and amphibians—when he convinced his mother to allow him to have a baby caiman (a relative of the alligator) as a pet. That and family visits to Florida, where he encountered lots of lizards, set the course for his career. He earned his degrees from Harvard University and the University of California, Berkeley. He was a professor at Washington University in Saint Louis and Harvard, and now he teaches and researches again at Washington U. He also directs the Living Earth Collaborative, a biodiversity partnership among the university, the Saint Louis Zoo, and the Missouri Botanical Garden. In his spare time, Jonathan hangs out with his other favorite animals, cats, and enjoys hiking, reading, traveling, and sports.

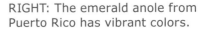
RIGHT: The emerald anole from Puerto Rico has vibrant colors.

A young Jonathan Losos shows off his new pet.

Jonathan Losos got hooked on anoles when, at eight years old, he captured a native green anole in Miami. "I go way back with them. I've been studying anoles ever since," he said. With eighth- and twelfth-grade science projects on anoles, and another when he was a senior in college, it seemed he was fated to devote his career to their study. He earned a Ph.D. in zoology and became an ecologist at Harvard University, following up on the work of his predecessor, Dr. Ernest Williams.

Dr. Williams had named the ecomorphs by describing their physical traits, figuring that these traits helped them succeed in their different environments. Jonathan decided to test these assumptions scientifically. Did longer hind legs actually help the trunk-ground lizards jump far and run fast? Were large toepads really helpful in moving around among smooth leaf surfaces?

How best to do this? Stage a Lizard Olympics, of course! The results? Indeed, Jonathan determined that the bigger toepads of the crown-giant ecomorphs aided them in clinging to slippery surfaces. The longer hind legs of the trunk-ground ecomorphs helped them jump well and run

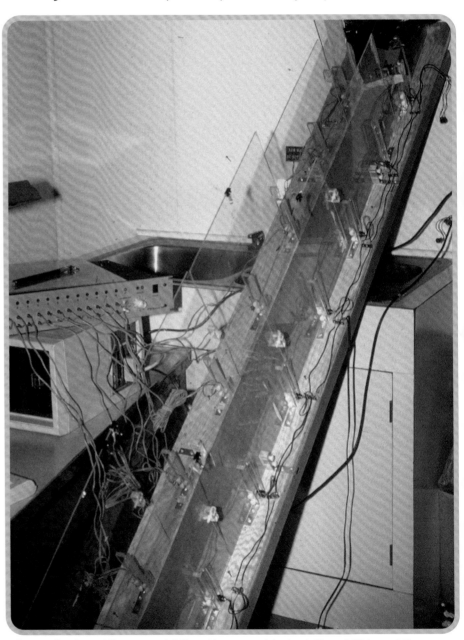

This is the lizard "racetrack" Jonathan used to test the abilities of the different anole ecomorphs on different surfaces.

faster, presumably enabling them to escape ground predators and to catch prey more effectively.

UNTANGLING RELATIONSHIPS

Now that Jonathan had established that the ecomorphs' differing physical traits could help them succeed in their specific habitats, he looked to evolution to study how these individuals had developed their useful adaptations over time.

"It's a detective story," he said. "I always compare evolution to a detective story. What happened in the past? The big question was: Did these ecomorphs evolve *once* and spread to the different islands, or did they evolve *separately* on each island?"

These sorts of questions were difficult to answer until the time came when scientists could easily analyze DNA. Using technological advancements made in the early 2000s for rapid DNA sequencing, researchers determined that the anoles on each of the four Greater Antilles islands evolved independently—with just one exception: the twig ecomorphs on Cuba and Hispaniola are closely related. That singularity aside, the DNA evidence confirms, for example, that the trunk-ground ecomorph on an island is more closely related to the crown-giant on that *same* island than it is to the trunk-ground ecomorphs on other

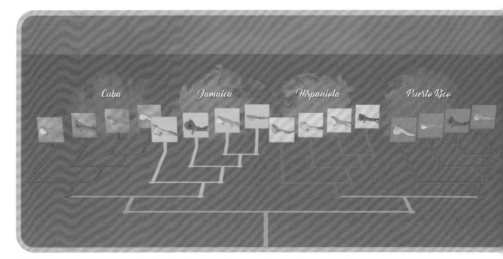

DNA shows that each of the four islands of the Greater Antilles has species of four ecomorphs. The lines show that way back in time, one species evolved into others that eventually became four species, each of which independently evolved over time into new species of four different ecomorphs on each island.

islands. The trunk-ground ecomorphs may look similar, but their DNA shows that *their appearance came about independently on each island*.

HOW DID THE DIFFERENT ECOMORPHS ARISE?

The four islands of the Greater Antilles have very similar conditions. They are close enough to one another to have the same climate. All of them have big trees, bushes, some open ground, and a variety of insects, spiders, and other anole food items. Long ago, a different ancestor species of anole arrived by chance on each island, and each island had almost identical conditions.

At first there were a few similar lizards with lots of choices about where to settle down. As time passed, the anole populations increased. With more competition, finding food and avoiding predators became harder. The various habitats on each island had different challenges for the lizards.

Bit by bit, generation after generation, the most successful individuals on the ground—those with long hind legs that allowed them to run fast and coloring that helped them hide—contributed more offspring to the next generation. Gradually, over many generations, anoles living on the ground became distinct from the others.

Meanwhile, other anoles found their place among the trees, where they could avoid predators that lived on the ground. But other predators, like birds and some snakes, can hunt in the trees. The lizards that blended in well with their background—brown ones on the trunks and green ones among the leaves—were able to survive and reproduce better than those that were more visible.

Some came to live low on the tree trunks, evolving strong legs to use in jumping to the ground to capture prey. Others became better at moving among smooth leaves using their bigger toepads. The green lizards that matched the color of the leaves were harder for predators to find, so they had a better chance of leaving offspring that lived in their green, leafy habitat. The parallel evolution of these different species on each island took many generations (an anole generation time is about one year) over a long time span.

The changes came about through small, random mutations in the genes that added up bit by bit as the lizards became better and better adapted to their different environments. Eventually the lizards on each island became distinct from one another and could mate only with others like themselves. On each island, the original pioneer species evolved slowly into different species adapted to their specific environment. Scientists call this process adaptive radiation.

FROM THEN TO NOW

Anole species evolved independently to live on each island of the Greater Antilles. Random events put a different anole ancestor on each island. Over the ages, new species evolved, developing traits that allowed each of them to succeed separately in a specific ecological niche. For example, traits that enable a lizard to survive and reproduce while making its home in the treetops are basically the same on each island. So on each island, crown-giants with green color and big toepads evolved from the ancestor. Trunk-ground species that hang out on the lower part of the tree trunks waiting for prey evolved separately with their brown

This rare piece of amber encasing an anole that died about twenty million years ago shows that these lizards have been adapting to the island environments for a very long time.

colors, small toepads, and strong hind legs.

So it's really no surprise that the crown-giant species on each island looks like the crown-giants inhabiting the other islands. Their ancestors' camouflaging green color and bigger toepads that could cling more securely to slippery leaves provided a better chance of surviving in the treetops. The same process also resulted in species in other habitats that resemble one another on each island. That's called convergent evolution.

CHAPTER FOUR
A FIELD BIOLOGIST AT WORK

Dr. James Stroud

James Stroud is a postdoctoral research associate in Jonathan Losos's lab at Washington University in St. Louis. Originally from England, James decided that he'd served his time in the rain, and after he finished his master's degree, he made a move to sunnier climes, earning his Ph.D. at Florida International University.

James writes of the study under way during my visit in Miami: "My research project at Fairchild Gardens studies 4 (now 5) species where I attempt to catch, measure, and mark all lizards on an island area in the Garden. I then re-survey the community every 6 months to catch, measure, and mark all the lizards and see which lizards have made it through the previous season. It's the first ever study of natural selection of 3+ lizard species living in one community at the same time. I have been conducting this study every 6 months since October 2015, making it one of the longest continually sampled projects of natural selection in the world."

As his research continues over time, James's love of lizards combines with his fascination with evolutionary biology.

James takes a break after successfully catching the anole he's gently holding.

RIGHT: The bark anole lives on James's research site.

Watching scientists at work always impresses me when I see their devotion, focus, and determination to uncover the mysteries of the natural world. They will brave stormy weather, hordes of mosquitoes, and long, frustrating hours when nothing goes right. After that, it takes hours of detailed work in the lab that requires great concentration and careful accuracy in order to capture the data they need to unravel how nature functions. The rewards are more than worth the discomforts.

I wanted to learn firsthand how James acquires data for showing how a community of anoles lives together. In his study area, James works with the species currently living there to understand how a lizard's chosen habitat has an impact on its survival over time.

When he began, just four kinds of anoles were present. The native green anole lived along with three nonnative species—the brown (trunk-ground ecomorph) and knight (crown-giant) anoles from Cuba, and bark (trunk

These five anole species now all live in Miami. The largest is the knight anole. Top right is the bark anole, then the native green species, with the brown anole right below it and the crested anole in the lower left. The crested is the most recent addition to the group at James's site, brought there by Hurricane Irma in 2017.

ecomorph) anoles from Hispaniola. Before the nonnative species arrived, the native green anole had free rein of the environment, spending time on the ground and in bushes and trees, free of interference from any other anole species. Now it spends more time in the trees, choosing a high-rise lifestyle to avoid confrontations with brown and bark anoles that live lower down on the trees. The knight anole, much bigger than the others, spends most of its time among the large branches up high, not moving around very much.

In 2017, Hurricane Irma tore across Florida. Alongside the destruction it left in its path, Irma carried yet another species onto James's island, the trunk-ground crested anole, originally from Puerto Rico. Suddenly this community became home to two trunk-ground ecomorphs, the Puerto Rican newbie and the resident brown anole, placing them in competition for territory.

How are they responding to these challenges? The generation time of anoles is about one to two years, so it might be possible to uncover changes in their behavior or their bodies that help ease competition between species.

Situations like this have rarely been studied by scientists, for they don't often happen in nature. Since James had already been gathering data on how the four resident species divided up the environment, he now has a special opportunity to follow any changes in these two trunk-ground ecomorphs (brown and crested) as a result of their competition for similar habitats.

James's research site features trees and bushes that make good homes for the anoles that live there.

COLLECTING THE DATA

James and his assistant, Kamau Walker, like to head out early in the morning, hunting the lizards on the island with tiny lassos attached to slender extendable fishing poles.

By the time I arrive to join James and Kamau in midmorning, they've already been busy for hours, snagging anoles. Sneaking up on a perched lizard is tricky, as these animals are always on alert for predators. I watch James as he ducks this way and that, carefully poking his head among the tree branches, intently seeking out these evasive lizards.

James spots one perched high, slowly inches his elongated pole up, and positions the loop in front of the lizard. Then, in a flash,

James finds an anole on a branch above and carefully positions his pole with the loop so he can capture the lizard.

he jerks the lasso over the unsuspecting creature as the loop closes around its neck.

He removes the struggling lizard carefully and gives it a quick once-over to make sure it hasn't already been captured during that research period (a dot of paint marks the lizard as already caught this season; it comes off when the lizard molts, shedding its old skin). It's a new find, so he slips it into an air-filled plastic bag marked with the time and the place where it was found.

The location on the bush or tree is labeled with a colored ribbon so the lizard can be returned home the next morning after being measured and photographed in the lab. When it gets too hot for the lizards—and the people—to be moving around, James and Kamau head to the lab while I go to the garden café for a quick lunch.

James removes a captured native green anole from the loop.

He checks on the lizard within the safety of an inflated plastic bag that he will take back to the lab.

James ties a ribbon around the spot where the lizard was found so he can return it there the next day after taking its measurements.

It doesn't take long before the trees and bushes in the study area are marked with colorful "lizard ribbons."

RECORDING THE DATA

Afternoon is lab time. When I arrive after lunch, James and Kamau are busy recording every detail they can about each lizard. Each one gets weighed, and all its parts are measured. How long is its body? How wide is its head? How long are its legs? How about its toepads (these get photographed in magnification)?

Kamau Walker takes a photo of the lizard's foot so he can measure the toepad size. When he has the lizard positioned just the way he wants it, he uses a cell phone linked to the computer to take the photo.

James takes a snippet from the end of the lizard's tail and preserves it in alcohol so that its DNA can be analyzed. Lizards' tails come off easily when a predator takes a bite, so taking just the tip for analysis is probably painless. James slips a tiny tag—with a unique code, only readable using a special UV black light—under the lizard's translucent skin so it can be easily identified when caught again.

Is the lizard in good health? Is it male or female? How old is it? Most survive only one to two years, rarely longer. The scientists work exceptionally hard to find and catch every single lizard on the island, so if one doesn't show up, chances are it died during the last six months.

James gently holds one of the anoles to note the labels that show its file number. By labeling each individual, he can keep track of it over time.

All the measurements become part of a database. Analyzing the data can help identify what traits are most important for survival in the conditions where the lizards live. James and Kamau pursue the goal of catching every lizard and accurately recording the detailed information with precision and patience. One reason I chose not to become a university scientist was because I knew I wouldn't be patient enough for this kind of work. I'm grateful for scientists like James and the other lizard scientists who gather the information needed to help further study.

ADAPTING TO SHARED HABITAT

At James's study site, he has the unique opportunity to study how the brown and crested anoles adapt to one another over time. These two species have shared their habitat in other parts of Miami for many years. In those other areas, the brown anoles tend to perch lower on the trees and spend more time on the ground to avoid competing with the crested anoles. Similarly, the crested anoles also try to avoid brown anoles by hanging out higher on the tree trunks than they do when not sharing habitat. Physical changes in the brown anoles living elsewhere with the crested species have also evolved. Their legs are longer than those of brown anoles that live higher in the trees when crested anoles aren't present.

James's data will record any changes in both the behavior and structure of these two species on this particular island now that they share the space. Will these brown anoles come to live lower on the trees, like those in other areas that they share with the crested species? If so, will those that happen to have longer legs be more likely to survive and reproduce, as they can move faster on the ground where predators might hunt? Will physical changes—like longer legs—appear in the lizards James examines? Time will tell if these changes occur, as anoles' short generation time could allow James to document them over time. The Covid-19 pandemic temporarily interrupted his

A male brown anole expands his dewlap and claims this spot as his territory on James's research site. Will James be able to record changes in these lizards now that they are sharing their habitat with another trunk-ground species, the crested anole?

research, but didn't end it. The work will continue when it's okay to travel again. Also, he just became a father for the first time, so that's been keeping him home on paternity leave!

LIZARDS ON THE LOOSE

Anole researchers want to know where anoles coming in from the Antilles and Bahamas are managing to settle and survive in city environments. The Miami area is now home to six species—native green anoles, brown and knight anoles from Cuba, crested anoles from Puerto Rico, bark anoles from Hispaniola, and giant anoles from Jamaica. Where do they live? How abundant are they? How do they divide the various habitats in different parts of this large metropolitan area? No one scientist or group of scientists could possibly collect enough data to even consider these questions.

Luckily, there's help—in the form of Lizards on the Loose, a program sponsored by the Fairchild Challenge, an environmental science competition managed by the Fairchild Tropical Botanic Garden.

Students from schools throughout southern Florida take photos with their smartphones of the lizards they discover in their schoolyards and around their homes. All smartphone pictures automatically record detailed GPS data of where the lizard photo was taken. Students then upload the picture to the online Lizards on the Loose website that is part of the citizen science program iNaturalist.

Project leaders James Stroud and Chris Thawley help students identify the species of lizard in each picture. During the 2018-19 school year, more than one hundred middle school students from eighteen schools recorded more than

Jose Marti MAST 6–12 Academy has an arboretum that provides perfect habitats for anoles.

James answers a question about an anole as he goes through the audience at a community meeting.

thirty-five hundred sightings of anoles throughout the Greater Miami area. The brown anole was by far the most common species spotted.

I visited the Jose Marti MAST 6-12 Academy in North Miami to meet some sixth-grade Lizards on the Loose student-scientists and see them in action. The school has a beautiful arboretum—a garden of native trees—that is a great environment for anoles.

While the students hunted for lizards, phones and cameras ready, I chatted with teacher Erik Veiga by the

For the Lizards on the Loose project, these students are hunting for anoles to photograph in the arboretum at the school. Each photo is automatically marked with its location and other information.

arboretum. Then a girl came up to us, held out her hand, and asked, "Is this an egg?"

Indeed, it was an anole egg about the size of a large green pea, but white in color. I'd been hoping to see an anole egg during my trip, and here one was right in front of me, discovered by students. Two girls showed me where they'd uncovered the egg—in a depression on a rough brick. Anoles have clearly made this place their home.

I joined the students as they poked their heads into bushes and craned their necks to look at the upper tree branches. Their phones and cameras clicked often, gathering information that can help scientists study the occurrence of various species of lizards, along with their habitats, in the city.

Through this program, the students discover how anoles use urban environments in the Greater Miami region.

The information they gather can help answer questions such as:

> • Do city lizards limit themselves to living in the natural environment such as shade trees and parks? Or are city anoles adapting to life on human-made surfaces such as the walls of buildings, power poles, and fences? How widespread are the various species of nonnative anoles in the urban area?

Data collected by Lizards on the Loose student-scientists represents the world's biggest study investigating the urban ecology of lizards. As the students document the lizards with their photos, project leaders James and Chris continue to monitor the spread of nonnative anoles through the Miami area. The students have already provided lots of new and useful information, including finding some populations of crested anoles that even the scientists hadn't yet known about!

This little white ball is actually an anole egg of unknown species that was laid in the arboretum at the Jose Marti MAST 6–12 Academy campus. The students were excited about their find.

CHAPTER FIVE
ISLAND TEST TUBES

Dr. Jason Kolbe

Jason Kolbe carefully adjusts his camera to take a photo of an anole from below.

Jason Kolbe is an associate professor in the Department of Biological Sciences at the University of Rhode Island. An evolutionary ecologist, he studies many aspects of anole life on research islets in The Bahamas. Jason says, "I'm mostly interested in how global change is driving evolutionary change—things like climate change, urbanization, and invasive species. I like working with great colleagues and students on challenging research questions, traveling to interesting locations in the Caribbean and South Florida, feeling like I can answer any question in ecology and evolution with anoles—and, last but not least, I love catching lizards!"

Dr. Rob Pringle

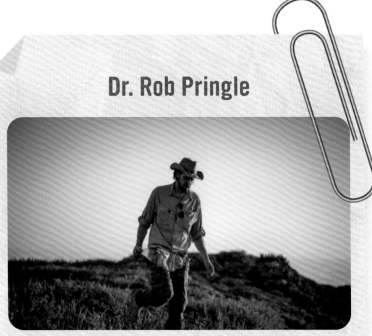

Rob Pringle on the hunt for anoles in The Bahamas.

Rob Pringle, a biologist at Princeton University, studies how anole species interact with one another. For example, how do the separate species divide up the available food and territory in environments they share? Rob writes, "What I love most about anoles is that they provide a beautiful opportunity to study some of the most important unsolved mysteries in ecology and evolutionary biology."

By studying anoles under natural conditions, he hopes to learn how multiple closely related species are able to coexist in the same place, despite competing with one another.

RIGHT: Brown anoles are common in many areas.

The adaptive radiation into the ecomorphs on the Greater Antilles took millions of years. But is it possible to follow how these reptiles become modified in the short term? If their environment changes, can anoles begin to adapt quickly enough that scientists can actually track these changes and study evolution in action?

STUDYING EXTINCTION, FINDING SURVIVAL

In the mid-1970s, ecologist Dr. Thomas Schoener and his wife, biologist Dr. Amy Schoener, wanted to study how species became extinct. Anoles, with their short generation time, were perfect subjects, and the Bahamian island chain north of the Greater Antilles provided an ideal variety of environments. The Bahamas consists of more than seven hundred islands, but also countless tiny islets, officially called "rocks." These islets have simple ecosystems that vary with their size. Some have trees, others don't. Some have lots of small shrubs while others are little more than a pile of rocks with a few small plants.

Jason Kolbe at work in the field.

The Bahamas has thousands of small islets like these, with different sizes and amounts of vegetation. You can see in this group that the size and vegetation are similar on some islets and have basically the same conditions—like separate test tubes in a rack in a laboratory.

The scientists selected lizardless islets of various sizes and introduced five or ten native Bahamian brown anoles to each islet, all from the same nearby and larger island.

The Schoeners checked on the lizards for five years. As they expected, those on the tiniest rocks, which lacked sufficient resources, died off quickly, while the populations on somewhat larger islets took longer to fail. But surprisingly, anoles on islets with even a small amount of vegetation could survive and even thrive in some cases. Why, then, were there no anoles on these islets already? When the Schoeners published their results, they suggested that catastrophic events, likely hurricanes, had probably wiped out any earlier anole populations. After wrapping up this study, the Schoeners moved on to other experiments. Without realizing it, they had set up the process for further studies, ones dealing not with extinction, but rather with evolution.

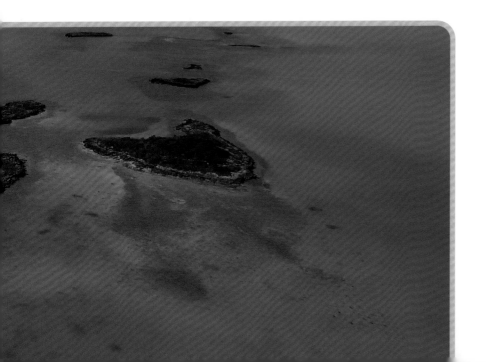

TRACING EVOLUTION AS IT HAPPENS

Fast-forward to the early 1990s, when graduate student Jonathan Losos was studying how different anole species adapted to different habitats. He read the Schoeners' paper and wondered what had happened to the island anole populations since the end of the Schoeners' study fourteen years earlier. Had the lizards changed in ways that could be measured?

The original anoles the Schoeners used came from Staniel Cay, a big island with trees. Could the descendants of the long-legged, tree-living anoles relocated to treeless islets that had only bushes have already evolved shorter limbs to better get around in this new environment? And would the descendants of those that were relocated to the islets *with* trees have long legs like their ancestors? Jonathan wondered whether evolution could work quickly enough for him to actually observe and measure it.

In 1991, Jonathan joined the Schoeners' yearly field trip to The Bahamas to capture lizards from the experimental islets and measure their legs. After analyzing the collected data, he found that the descendants of anoles introduced to islets with broad vegetation were long-legged, like their ancestors. Conversely, descendants of anoles introduced to islets with slender-branched vegetation had shorter legs.

The species were adapting to new environments within fourteen years. Evolution *could* be observed as it occurred!

The publication of these results in the British scientific journal *Nature* was announced in a press release stating "This may be among the most important work in evolutionary studies since Darwin studied the diversity of finches on the Galapagos Islands during the voyage of the *Beagle*." Suddenly Jonathan Losos was in the first section of the *New York Times*, on the front page of the *Boston Globe*, and in *USA Today*. His work was even mentioned in an ABC News report on television! Not only other scientists, but the public could learn the importance of this work.

The scientific community responded to Losos's findings with excitement. Now there are actually ways to investigate a basic question about evolution: Did life on Earth evolve as it did largely by accident, or do the conditions in the environment determine the physical and behavioral characteristics of living things even down to the details? The independent evolution of the anole ecomorphs in the Greater Antilles provided evidence for how intense evolutionary pressure can be over millions of years. Now scientists realized that they could follow how these changes happened bit by bit under experimental conditions.

Some islands have lots of trees.

The Bahamas quickly became an important site for studying evolution in action. As Jonathan points out, "If you locate small enough islands so that you can study a whole population, yet big enough that the anoles can survive and adapt, each island is almost the equivalent of a laboratory test tube."

Having a "control" in a scientific experiment is important. These scientists left a group of similar islets alone while changing the conditions on others. Then they compared the unchanged "control" and the islets with changes,

just as in a lab with test tubes. For example, in a laboratory, to test whether a chemical kills a particular kind of bacteria, you might have a series of test tubes to which you add different concentrations of the chemical. You would also include at least one test tube that did not have any of the chemical added. That way you could measure each of the experimental tubes in comparison with the original situation.

Jonathan and his colleagues set to work. They took a sample of brown anoles from a big island with broad trunk trees and moved them to seven small islets with brushy, narrow-stemmed vegetation. The scientists checked on the lizards every year, and they detected physical changes just four years after introduction. The hind legs of the lizards on the big island with trees (the control) were still the same as those of their ancestors. But the anoles on all seven islets where there were no trees had significantly shorter hind legs than their tree-adapted ancestors. Natural selection could be measured in just *four* years!

EVOLVING BEHAVIOR

Once these scientists realized that they could get meaningful results so quickly, they began using the Bahamian islets for other studies.

Could they identify changes in behavior—as well as in leg length? How would anoles behave in the presence of a predator such as the large, powerful curly-tailed lizard—a ground-dwelling carnivore that eats other lizards and inhabits many Bahamian islands but not others? It's twice as long and weighs ten times as much as a brown anole.

In this experiment, more than one question was being asked: Would the presence of the predator on the experimental islands change the anoles' behavior so they'd be spending more time in the bushes to avoid being eaten? And since longer legs help them run faster, would more anoles with longer legs survive?

In April 1997, the researchers chose twelve bushy islets that had brown anoles but no curly-tails. Then they divided the islets up into six similar pairs. To make sure the choices for controls and experimental islets for each pair were random, a coin toss determined which one would get curly-tails and which would be a control. Before adding the predators, the scientists measured the leg lengths of virtually all the brown anoles. Then they added five curly-tails to one islet in each pair and left the other six islets as controls.

When the scientists checked six months later, they found

Researchers arrive at an island with lots of bushes and trees.

that islets with curly-tails had half as many anoles as the controls. The curly-tails had been enjoying a feast! In addition, the behavior of the surviving anoles had changed. They spent only about 10 percent of the time on the ground, while those on the control islets with no curly-tails were found on the ground about 33 percent of the time, the same as before the experiment began. The scientists kept checking on the lizards, and as time passed, this difference increased. After two years, the anoles on islets with curly-tails were perching seven times higher than those on control islands.

Researchers search for anoles on an island with no trees, only bushes.

The researchers also noticed that even though the bush-climbing lizards were less likely to become victims of the curly-tails, they moved clumsily around on the narrow bush branches. Their long, strong legs, good for running and jumping, weren't that good for moving about in the bushes. Would this new difficulty result in a reversal in natural selection, so that anoles with shorter legs would have a better chance of surviving to reproduce and therefore pass on that trait to their offspring?

The hopeful scientists waited to see what would happen over the years on these islets. But yet again, nature cut the experiment short as Hurricane Floyd struck in September 1999, submerging the islets in its storm surge for hours and washing away the lizards. End of experiment.

The curly-tailed lizard is big, powerful, and hungry!

IF AT FIRST YOU DON'T SUCCEED, TRY AGAIN

By 2003, the vegetation and anole populations had replenished enough for a new set of experiments, again using the resident brown anoles (their eggs in the ground had survived and hatched to jump-start new populations) and the addition of the curly-tailed predators. This time, however, the anoles were measured in detail and individually marked so they could be followed over time.

After just six months, as in the earlier experiment, the anoles with longer hind legs were surviving better in the presence of curly-tails than those with shorter hind limbs. And the longer the anoles' legs were, the greater their chance for survival. Natural selection had again favored anoles with longer hind limbs. And as before, the surviving anoles were spending more time up in the bushes to get away from the ground-dwelling curly-tail predators.

The scientists waited to see if the long-legged anoles' new bush habitat created enough problems so that natural selection would reverse itself and favor shorter limbs that would work better for moving among the narrow branches.

In May 2004, a year after the experiment began, this reversal in natural selection had already begun—even more quickly than the scientists had expected. Shorter-legged anoles were surviving better. But to show actual evolutionary change over generations, the scientists needed to follow the lizards for years to see if shorter legs would become the norm on the curly-tail-inhabited islands. Unfortunately, *two* powerful hurricanes swept through The Bahamas in September 2004, swamping out the lizards and the experiment.

Luckily, scientists don't let hurricanes stop them. They continue to work with anoles on the islands, devising ever more complex experiments to understand interactions on even the smallest and simplest islets. The anole researchers find new ways to use these so-called blank-slate islands as they work to tease apart the many threads that make up not only the evolution of lizard species but also the evolution of the ecosystems in which they live.

If an anole isn't fast enough, the curly-tailed lizard can capture it and eat it.

LIZARD SPECIES INTERACTIONS

Trunk-crown green anoles can share a habitat with such trunk-ground anoles as the brown anole. And we know that adding curly-tailed lizards can alter the way brown anoles behave, forcing them to spend more time in trees and bushes than they did before this ground-dwelling predator appeared. But what if all three species had to live together on the same small island? How would the two species of anoles adjust their behavior, since their tree-dwelling habitats overlap?

Rob Pringle, Jason Kolbe, Jonathan Losos, and other scientists worked together to design and carry out a major experiment starting in 2011. They chose sixteen similar Bahamian islets that were already home to brown anoles and tall vegetation.

The scientists did their best to count the number of brown anoles on each islet so they knew what the populations were before starting the experiment.

Then they randomly divided the islets into groups of four. They left four islets alone as controls, with just the resident brown anoles. On four other islets they introduced ten green trunk-crown anoles. This allowed them to see what might happen naturally, since the green anole species is native to this area and could end up on an islet by chance. On four other islets, they added six curly-tailed lizards. On the last four islets, both the green *and* the curly-tailed lizards were added to see how the stress of an additional predator would affect the anoles. The scientists now had the technology to analyze the DNA in the lizards' poop, so they could see what each lizard species had been eating. All three species feed mainly on insects and spiders. How much did their diets overlap? And did the curly-tails also eat the anoles?

For five years, the experimenters checked on the islets, counting the populations of the lizard species and, in order to uncover their diet, analyzing DNA from whatever poop they could find. Here's what they found:

Control islets: The population of brown anoles increased an average of 177 percent, with no competition and no predator.

Islets with green anoles added: The brown anoles increased an average of 40 percent when having to compete for habitat with the greens. The greens went from 10 per islet to 55 to 161, able to adapt and increase their populations while sharing habitat with the browns. The brown anoles didn't change their behavior much when the greens were added, except that they spent a bit more time on the ground than before.

Islets with only curly-tails added: The populations of brown anoles stayed about the same. They were able to maintain their numbers, but not increase them. They spent much less time on the ground than before, avoiding the curly-tails as much as possible.

Islets with both curly-tails and greens added: The brown populations went down by 42 percent. The greens died off completely on two of the islets, increased a bit on one, and stayed the same on the fourth.

The diets of the two insect eaters differed, showing

Results of Lizard Species Interactions Experiment

Control Islets: only resident brown anoles	Experimental Group #1: resident browns + green trunk- crown species	Experimental Group #2: curly tails added to resident browns	Experimental Group #3: resident browns + green trunk-crown anoles + curly tails

Results after 5 years: Brown anole population increased on average 177% with no predator and no added green trunk-crown lizards.	Results after 5 years: Greens adapted well. Their population on each islet increased from 10 to an average of 90 individuals. Browns spent a bit more time on the ground than on the control islets.	Results after 5 years: With curly-tails added, the population of browns stayed about the same. They spent less time on the ground, avoiding curly-tails as much as possible.	Results after 5 years: With both green and curly-tails added, the brown population dropped by 42%. The greens died off completely on two of the four islets, stayed the same on one islet, and increased a bit on one.

KEY: Brown Anole   Green Anole   Curly-tail Lizard

49

that they weren't competing that much for food when the browns were able to spend time on the ground safely.

With the curly-tails added, however, things got more complicated. The brown anoles were pressured by their fear to stay on the trees as much as possible. They began to force the greens upward and compete more for food and space. The brown anoles' fear of the predator became a strong ecological influence. The greens themselves weren't directly threatened by the curly-tails, but the threat of the predator to the brown anoles made the browns suppress the greens with dewlap displays and aggressive behavior that forced the greens to reduce their own habitat. The greens couldn't carve out enough space to survive.

When we think about the evolution of anoles into the different ecomorphs, it's important to remember that, as the researchers say, "Lizards are nature's lunch boxes" —just about any predator can make a snack of an anole. Fear of being eaten can be an important factor that influences an animal's behavior. Over the generations, behavioral changes such as fleeing into the trees can affect physical traits such as leg length and can even affect the welfare of a species not itself threatened by a predator, as this experiment shows.

The green anoles had a completely different diet from the curly-tails. They also weren't significantly threatened by them, since they live up in the trees and the curly-tails live down on the ground. But the pressure of fear that

motivated the brown anoles led to forcing the greens higher up the trees, where they might have trouble finding enough to eat. This difficulty kept the greens from being able to establish populations when the curly-tails were present.

Speedy movement and color patterns that blend into the environment are critical to survival for these animals. Think about this: you're walking along a forest path and see a quick rustling in the dead leaves, then nothing. You know something was there, and chances are it was a lizard. But where is it? Rustle the leaves yourself, and you'll see another quick disturbance, then nothing. The lizard may be visible, but it's so well disguised by its color pattern that it blends in completely. The same is true for tree-dwelling lizards. With its gray-brown pattern and flattened body, a trunk anole that's not moving is very difficult to see on a tree. A bright green lizard among bright green tropical leaves? It's also a challenge to locate. Surviv-

This anole from the Dominican Republic blends in well with the green leaves around it.

al for a lizard is not an easy task, but natural selection over time has produced well-adapted species that can change quickly through a few generations to thrive as the environment changes.

The mixed dark colors on this anole from Central America make it hard to see on the dark tree trunk.

CHAPTER 6
OF HURRICANES AND TOEPADS

Dr. Colin Donihue

Colin Donihue holds a snake from the island of Antigua.

Colin Donihue's work on the ecology and evolution of lizards has taken him to four continents so far. As a postdoctoral fellow in Jonathan Losos's lab, he studied many different aspects of anole biology. But when Hurricane Irma hit a study site in 2017, his research took a surprising turn to focus on species evolving in response to extreme climate events. Colin says, "My favorite anole research trip was to a remote island in the Leeward Islands chain of the West Indies—it's uninhabited, with cliffs so steep we had to get there by helicopter! I spent a week camping, without electricity, to get data on an endangered anole species that can only be found on that little island." Colin's love of remote islands and rare anoles led to other research that turned out to have perfect timing for fascinating results.

RIGHT: Storm clouds gather over the Caribbean.

The earth is experiencing rising temperatures, more severe storms, and less reliable weather. How might such changes affect the biodiversity of our planet? Scientists can't always plan experiments that depend on natural events like hurricanes to learn how living things might adapt and survive. But now and then, they can take advantage of a situation or dig into existing data that might give hints about what the future could hold.

Anoles' small size may make them potential lizard lunches, but it also allows them to avoid some extreme circumstances more easily than larger animals can. Their short generation time of a year or two provides an opportunity for quick adaptation to changes in the environment.

SEVERE STORMS

We've seen scientists work hard to set up long-term studies in The Bahamas, only to have them wiped out by hurricanes that plague the region. Still, if scientists are in the right place at the right time, hurricanes can provide opportunities to ask different research questions.

In 2017, a group of anole scientists, including Dr. Colin Donihue, traveled to the Turks and Caicos Islands to study an anole *(Anolis scriptus)* that is endemic to this string of islands, meaning that it isn't found anywhere else in the world.

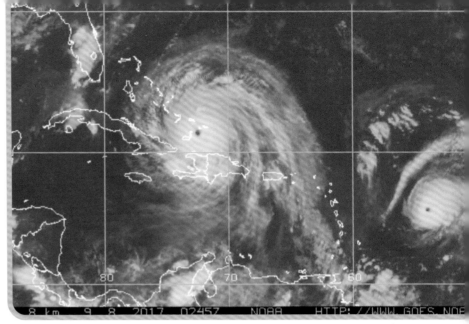

The eye of Hurricane Irma, in the center of the photo, is about to hit the islands Colin is studying on September 8, 2017.

This rare anole is found only on the Turks and Caicos Islands.

Colin's assistant searches for anoles before Hurricane Irma arrives.

After a week of intense catching, measuring, and filming these lizards, the scientists departed. Four days later, the eye of Category 5 Hurricane Irma passed directly over the area, lashing these small islands with winds up to 265 kph (164 mph). Two weeks after that, Hurricane Maria struck. Maria's winds were hardly less punishing, with sustained winds of 200 kph (124 mph). The scientists realized that they had a rare opportunity to discover whether the lizards that survived this onslaught had traits that helped them do so.

Nature had accidentally carried out a potential experiment for them.

Six weeks after their first visit, Colin and his colleague Dr. Anthony Herrel returned to the battered islands to capture the surviving anoles. Would they show any measurable traits that had helped them survive?

Hurricane Irma tore apart the vegetation on this island, making it hard for the returning scientists to find the remaining lizards.

The researchers hypothesized that if there were any traits that advantaged the surviving lizards, one might be larger toepads, which would help them cling to surfaces in the strong winds. They also predicted that the anoles' front and hind legs would be longer to help them hang on to branches.

Indeed, more lizards with bigger toepads had survived the blasting winds than those with smaller ones. The scientists tested the toepads' ability to cling and confirmed that larger toepads did a better job.

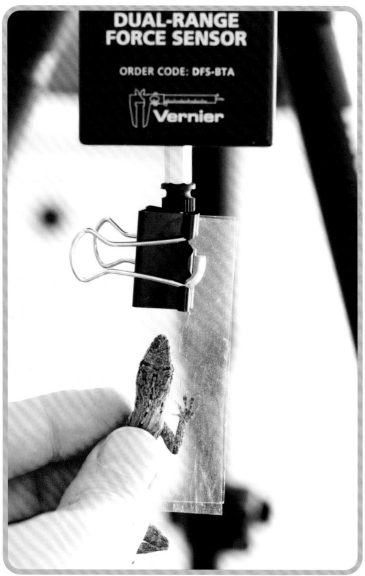

Colin uses this device to determine the clinging ability of the lizard's toepads.

As expected, these anoles also tended to have longer front limbs. Both of the two islands studied showed the same pattern, strengthening the case that the storms had shifted the traits of the lizards in the same way.

A surprise came when the scientists measured the survivors' hind legs. They actually tended to be *shorter* than the average recorded before the hurricanes struck, especially the thighs. What was going on? Wouldn't longer, stronger legs help the lizards cling to the trees and not get blown away by the incredibly strong hurricane winds? It was time for another experiment to try to ascertain how these lizards behaved in strong winds.

To explore this unexpected discovery, Colin and his colleagues brought in the strongest leaf blower they could find and tested the lizards' grip against the wind. They filmed about forty anoles with different leg lengths to see which ones lasted longest as the wind speed increased.

While the lizards started out holding on with their arms and legs, as the air from the blower sped up, it struck the lizards' thighs, which then acted like sails, catching the wind and flinging the bodies outward until the front limbs lost their grip and the lizards were blown into the safety net. The shorter hind limbs had less surface area, which may have made it more likely that lizards with shorter hind legs could hang on better and withstand the hurricane-force winds.

This illustration, showing different lizards trying to hang on in the wind, demonstrates the importance of testing ideas with experiments. The experimenters tested how the lizards' legs functioned in a strong wind. It would seem that longer, stronger legs would help the lizards cling to a support better in a strong wind. But the hind legs actually didn't help the lizards hang on; they lost their grip quickly, so larger hind legs could actually have been a problem by catching the wind like sails instead of helping the lizards withstand the wind better. The large numbers on the apparatus indicate the wind speed in miles per hour.

A native green anole in Miami.

CHECKING THE NEXT GENERATION

Colin and his colleagues traveled to the Turks and Caicos Islands eighteen months after their first revisit to measure whether the hurricane survivors had passed their traits on to the next generation. They found that the offspring of the survivors had basically the same measurements as their parents. It seems that bigger toepads could become a lasting shift in this important trait over many generations. The strength of hurricanes appears to be growing with climate change, so it's possible that larger toepads will be maintained as lizards who have them survive these storms better.

Drawing from this data, it is possible to guess that populations and species that have been hit by more hurricanes would tend to have larger toepads. To test the idea, Colin

needed to look at specimens of the widespread brown anole from various locations to see if toepad size was related to exposure to hurricanes over time.

Indeed, island populations of brown anoles that had been through more hurricanes had significantly larger toepads than those from areas with fewer hurricanes. So it seemed that the effect wasn't just in the Turks and Caicos.

This trunk-ground anole species now living in Miami is from the Domincan Repulbic.

This crown-giant from Puerto Rico also lives in Miami and is adaptiong to its new habitat.

Jonathan checks out the vast collection of preserved anoles at the Museum of Comparative Zoology, Harvard University.

What about anoles living in other locations affected frequently by hurricanes? Natural history museums are like a library for plants and animals, with millions of specimens preserved in their archives. Comparing the size of toepads for 188 anole species from around the entire Neotropics—from Florida all the way down to Brazil, across the big and small islands in the Caribbean and the mainland of Central America—showed that those living in areas with a history of more hurricanes had bigger toepads on both front and hind legs than those inhabiting places with fewer of these powerful storms.

Not only do big events bring about big changes in the lizards, these adaptations can carry into the future, helping anoles survive and even thrive in a world that keeps changing and becoming more extreme in those changes.

CHAPTER 7
COUNTRY LIZARD, CITY LIZARD

Dr. Kristin Winchell

For her Ph.D. research at the University of Massachusetts, Kristin Winchell examined the way anoles in Puerto Rico are adapting to life in urban areas. Now, as an Assistant Professor at New York University, she's investigating anoles in different cities to learn how they're adapting to urban conditions. For example, are they changing in the same ways as the lizards in Puerto Rico? And how about genetics—are the same genes involved when, say, brown anoles adapt to warmer temperatures in different places? Kristin writes about anoles, "I love that there are seemingly limitless possibilities of what you can study! They are also really fun to catch."

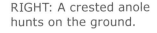

RIGHT: A crested anole hunts on the ground.

Dr. Shane Campbell-Staton

Shane Campbell-Staton undertook his Ph.D. research as a student of Jonathan Losos at Harvard University. He's now an assistant professor in the Department of Ecology & Evolutionary Biology at Princeton University, studying the effects of our changing climate and human disturbance on living things as diverse as lizards and elephants. He and Kristin Winchell have collaborated on projects that test the adaptive changes that have occurred as anoles move into urban environments. Shane's favorite species is the native green anole. He says, "I love the green anole. It's not as fancy as many other species, but it just has a special place in my heart as a southern boy. Plus, it's given me great opportunities to learn about evolution and the biological impacts of humans on the planet."

The majority of people in the world—about four billion—now live in cities rather than in the countryside, and the upward trend toward urban life continues. It's estimated that by 2050, two-thirds of people—close to seven billion—will live in urban areas. As cities get bigger, natural environments shrink, threatening wild species. Asphalt and concrete instead of grass and wildflowers, lampposts and power poles instead of trees and shrubs—these changes create environments called "urban heat islands" that are warmer than the surrounding natural landscape. Their less textured surfaces can be difficult for animals like lizards to move around on.

Urban areas such as San Juan, Puerto Rico, are taking over more and more wildlands. Wildlife like lizards needs to adapt to these new environments in order to survive.

Kristen erects her own Lizard Olympics setup to see if the city anoles have been developing adaptations to city life.

The biologist Kristin Winchell studies the ways in which the challenges of city life affect anoles. She captured native Puerto Rican crested anoles in cities and in the nearby forests to look for differences that help the lizards thrive in the city as well as in the countryside.

Even in the city, anoles can find homes in the landscaping around buildings and in parks, which provide plants and shade for them.

Inspired by Jonathan Losos's methods, Kristin held her own Lizard Olympics to determine whether these changes actually helped the city lizards survive. She tested the running speed of forest and city anoles on three surfaces—bark, painted concrete, and bare metal. The results showed that city lizards ran faster on the concrete and smooth metal than the country lizards, an adaptation that could help them survive city life.

Kristin tested this crested anole, a species native to Puerto Rico, to see how well it could climb smooth metal, hardly a natural surface, but found throughout the city.

Kristin Winchell and Shane Campbell-Staton hunt for anoles in the forest surrounding San Juan.

Shane watches a crested anole carefully as he raises the temperature to see how much heat the lizard can tolerate. He wants to be sure to cool it off as soon as it reaches the maximum heat it can manage. He's found that crested anoles that live in the city can stay active at higher temperatures than their forest relatives.

Meanwhile, Shane Campbell-Staton joined Kristin to test the heat tolerance of the lizards.

Lizards are cold-blooded, meaning that their body temperature depends on the environment. They can adjust their body temperature only through behavior—sunning to warm up, moving into shade to cool down. They can't cool off by sweating or any other internal means, making them especially susceptible to overheating. Shane tested heat tolerance by carefully raising the temperature around a lizard, then turning it on its back.

A lizard that could turn itself over onto its feet was able to function at that temperature. But when it could no longer turn over, Shane knew that the lizard had reached its limit, so he removed it and quickly cooled it down with a room-temperature water bath. After he tested many lizards from both the city and the forest, the results showed that urban lizards could tolerate a temperature one degree Celsius warmer than forest lizards. One degree doesn't sound like much, but it can make a huge difference in the life of a lizard that needs to hunt for food, escape danger, or find a mate, as opposed to being immobilized by hot temperatures or forced to stay still in a shady, cool location.

Climate change is affecting air temperatures around the world, with records breaking in many places every year. It's a hopeful finding that anoles have been able to adapt to a life in urban heat islands. But we don't know just how much increased temperature they can tolerate over time. We also don't know how other species might manage.

ANOLES AND CLIMATE CHANGE

Kristin and Shane delved deeper into the issue of anole adaptation to warmer environments by investigating whether they could detect genetic changes linked to the city anoles' ability to tolerate higher temperatures. Using the native crested anole in Puerto Rico as their subject, they headed up a study that tackled this question. Crested anoles inhabit both cities and the surrounding forests on the island. The cities are urban heat islands with average air temperatures higher in both summer and winter than in the forests. The scientists studied anoles from four different cities and their surrounding woods—Mayaguez, Aguadilla, Arecibo, and San Juan.

First they determined that the anole populations around each city evolved independently to adapt to the new, warmer environment as that city grew and took over parts of the forest. This meant that, within the same species, they had four different examples of separate adaptations to increased temperatures.

Then they looked at the genetics of each lizard group in detail. What genetic difference could they find between the city populations and the anoles living in the surrounding forests? Did all the city lizards show the same genetic adaptations to the warmer climate, or were they different?

The scientists found that the genes involved in making certain proteins differed in the city lizards from those of the forest populations. Natural selection had independently favored changes in the same region in each of the four different populations. This study is just the beginning of learning how some living things might adapt to the effects of increasing temperatures due to climate change. It also shows that separate populations of a particular species can adapt through the same genetic changes.

BECOMING "CITIFIED"

Physical traits such as heat tolerance and toepad size aren't the only factors that change for anoles in order for them to live successfully in the city. Cities aren't merely warmer, with different textured surfaces. The urban environment is more varied and unpredictable, with streets, parks, and buildings; cars, buses, and sirens; crowds of humans; bright and flashing lights. And sometimes city-dwelling anoles have to share their habitat with the curly-tailed predators. So it's not surprising that city lizards differ not only in their physical traits but also in their behavior.

Dr. Jason Kolbe and two other scientists decided to see if brown anoles living in cities reacted differently to unexpected activities in their environment than those inhabiting forests. They found that in cities where curly-tailed lizards lived, anoles left the safety of trees more in the mornings and evenings than in the middle of the day, when curly-tails are hunting. Anoles living without this predator spent more time off the trees during the day and tended to hang out lower than their cousins that shared their habitat with curly-tails. Those anoles with curly-tail neighbors also spend less time on the ground once they had captured prey than their cousins who lived in places without big, hungry predators.

We don't know if these behavior traits are developed by each lizard's experience or if they are inherited. This is a subject that researchers are just beginning to study. But it's clear that city anoles can be different in many ways from those in the surrounding wilds. Variations are a good thing, especially in a world that keeps changing as a result of human activities and the changing climate.

City lizards need to be able to adapt to environments that their ancestors never encountered in the wild.

RIGHT: A Jamaican gray anole displays his dewlap.

EPILOGUE

Many scientists predict that countless species will become extinct in the near future, particularly if human actions—such as destroying natural habitats, increasing carbon dioxide and other greenhouse gases in the atmosphere at the present rate, and not responding to the need to limit global warming with other policy changes—are not altered. Anoles are perfect subjects for studying how different species might adapt to changes in their environment. The conditions that make them so perfect for these studies, however, don't exist for most living things on Earth.

Small Size: Most anoles are no more than a foot long, including the tail. Small size has many advantages: Anoles can hide easily to protect themselves from predators or from dangerous conditions. They can exist in larger numbers, with more likelihood that some will survive stressful new conditions.

Jonathan holds a typical-size anole in Costa Rica.

Rapid Reproduction: They reproduce rapidly, with a generation time sometimes no more than a year. Individuals that can manage habitat changes long enough to breed and produce offspring have a chance to pass on their survival traits to the next generation.

Two American Chameleons (*A. carolinensis*) mate. The male is green, the female is brown. This highly successful and adaptable species is the only one native to North America. It survives and adapts to the presence of other anole species that have arrived from other places.

Varied Diet and Cold-Blooded: Anoles have a varied diet, consisting mostly of insects, spiders, small vertebrates, and, where available, nectar and fruit. If some of their food runs out, the remaining parts of their diet could keep them going. And being cold-blooded, they need only about one-tenth as much food as a warm-blooded animal to survive and be active.

If food is scarce, anoles are much more likely to survive than small, warm-blooded mammals, like shrews, that must eat two to three times their own weight each day! An anole can sunbathe on a rock to get warm and eat about a tenth as much as a shrew of the same size.

This Jamaican anole is chowing down on a worm.

A brown anole, probably the most successful species in the family, clings to the end of a broken branch against a blurred green background. As the world warms, will anoles be able to keep evolving fast enough to adapt to the changes?

As conditions change, a species with a large population consisting of modest-size individuals that can survive on a varied diet will have a better chance of keeping up with climate change than a big animal that breeds every few years and eats a narrow diet. It's also harder for the large animal to find a safe place to wait out a disaster, and it's not likely to breed fast enough to keep up with the changes in the environment.

Scientists who study anoles are fascinated by their variety, their beauty, their interesting behavior, and their value in exploring some of ecology's and evolution's big questions.

Even though the lifestyles of anoles, which favor adaptation, may not represent the possibilities of survival for larger and/or more specialized animals, we can still learn a great deal from these appealing creatures about possible ways of surviving on this rapidly changing planet. We all look forward to learning more from the lizard scientists about how nature works.

GLOSSARY

adaptive radiation: A process in evolution in which species change over time to fit into different habitats, resulting in new and different species.

anole: A lizard in the scientific family Anolidae.

Anolis: The genus name for members of the Anolidae, often abbreviated as *A.*

canopy: The top layer of a forest, where green leaves can get the most sunshine.

cold-blooded: A cold-blooded animal lacks the ability to use its own metabolism to warm its body. It needs warmth from outside its body to warm itself inside.

control (noun or adjective): In scientific experiments, when scientists test a new idea, in addition to the things they are changing to test the idea, they also keep one situation the same as it has been so they can compare the previous situation with the new one.

convergent evolution: Convergent evolution occurs when different species change over time to adapt to similar environments, resulting in similar appearance. For example, cactuses and some other plants called euphorbias have evolved thick green trunks, spines, and no leaves, which helps them survive in hot, dry places where animals might try to eat them.

Cuba: One of the Greater Antilles—four large islands in the Caribbean Sea.

dewlap: A loose flap of skin on the throat of male iguanas and anoles, also on some females. Anole dewlaps usually show bright colors.

Dominican Republic: One of two countries (the other is Haiti) on the island of Hispaniola, which is one of the Greater Antilles.

ecological niche: The role a living thing plays in the natural world.

ecology: The study of the interrelationships among living things in their different environments.

ecomorph: A set of physical traits—such as large toepads for clinging to leaves and long, strong hind legs for fast running—that help an animal survive in a particular habitat.

endemic: Native only to a particular geographic location.

evolution: In biology, the word *evolution* refers to the process of change over time that has led to the enormous variety of things living on Earth and adapted to different habitats.

generation time: The amount of time it takes on average between the birth of an individual and the birth of its offspring.

habitat: The kind of place where a living thing is naturally found.

Hispaniola: One of the four islands of the Greater Antilles. There are two countries on this island, Haiti and the Dominican Republic.

invasive species: A species that gets to a place where it doesn't occur naturally and survives and reproduces there. An invasive species can become a big problem when it multiplies and takes over a habitat.

Jamaica: One of the four islands of the Greater Antilles.

native (adjective): If a species is native, it is natural to a location, not an invasive species from somewhere else.

native green anole: The native green anole, *Anolis carolinensis*, is native to southeastern parts of the United States. It is the only U.S. native anole.

natural selection: The ecological process recognized and named by Charles Darwin in the nineteenth century. In natural selection, traits that allow an organism to survive and reproduce are passed on to the next generation, resulting in changes to the species over time. Scientist Alfred Wallace came to the same idea but didn't study and describe the process as Darwin did.

Neotropics: The region that includes the southern part of Mexico, Central and South America, and the islands of the Caribbean.

nonnative (adjective): A species that comes to a new environment from outside and survives there. Nonnative species often become problem invasive species, as they may have few or no natural enemies.

Puerto Rico: One of the four islands of the Greater Antilles. Puerto Rico is a territory of the United States but could become another state.

species: A biological classification of closely related individuals that can successfully breed only with others in the same classification. The word *species* is both singular and plural. Each species has its own scientific name.

The Bahamas: A Caribbean country north of the Greater Antilles consisting of thousands of islands of various sizes. The brown and a green anole species are native to The Bahamas. Scientists get permission to use the smaller islands there for experiments in anole adaption, evolution, and competition in order to understand how species change over time to survive in different habitats.

toepads: Expanded areas on the toes of anoles and geckos that help them cling to slippery surfaces.

TO LEARN MORE ABOUT ANOLES

I used these online sources to learn about these amazing lizards:

Online blog with recent research, comments, and photos: Anole Annals: www.anoleannals.org

The film *Laws of the Lizard*: www.smithsonianchannel.com/details/show/law-of-the-lizards

The Lizard's Tale videos:

   Episode 1—Introducing the Anoles: www.youtube.com/embed/iz1wlgWn8D0?v=iz1wlgWn8D0

   Episode 2—Does Evolution Repeat Itself?: www.youtube.com/watch?v=OCVEIgZ9JQQ

   Episode 3—Anoles in Deep Time: www.youtube.com/watch?v=LinZFAO2czI

   Episode 4—The Origin of Anole Species: www.youtube.com/watch?v=ysW8nvBQyFA

Scientists publish their work in journals and books devoted to research. Here are some select references:

Campbell-Staton, Shane, Kristin M. Winchell, et al. "Parallel Selection on Thermal Physiology Facilitates Repeated Adaptations of City Lizards to Urban Heat Islands. *Nature Ecology & Evolution* 4 (2020): 652-8

Donihue, Colin M., et al. "Hurricane Effects on Neotropical Lizards Span Geographic and Phylogenetic Scales." *PNAS* 117 (2020): 10429-34.

Donihue, Colin M., et al. "Hurricane-Induced Selection on the Morphology of an Island Lizard." *Nature* 560 (2018): 88-91.

Losos, Jonathan B. *Lizards in an Evolutionary Tree: Ecology and Adaptive Radiation of Anoles*. Berkeley: University of California Press, 2009.

I also consulted directly with the scientists through email and internet meetings. They all were very helpful and generous with their time, and I thank them enthusiastically for their help in creating this book.

SUGGESTED FURTHER READING

Collard, Sneed B. III. *One Iguana, Two Iguanas: A Story of Accident, Natural Selection, and Evolution*. Thomston, ME: Tilbury House Publishers, 2018.

This book for young readers describes how land iguanas and marine iguanas evolved on the Galapagos Islands long ago.

Hanson, Thor. *Hurricane Lizards and Plastic Squid: The Fraught and Fascinating Biology of Climate Change*. New York: Basic Books, 2021.

This book for the general public uses research on the effects of hurricanes on anoles as one example of how living things might be able to adapt to climate change.

Losos, Jonathan B. *Improbable Destinies: Fate, Chance, and the Future of Evolution*. New York: Riverhead Books, 2017.

Losos describes an assortment of research on evolution by various scientists including himself in this book for the general public.

PHOTO CREDITS

INDEX

Note: Page references in **bold** indicate photographs.

SCIENTISTS IN THE FIELD

WHERE SCIENCE MEETS ADVENTURE

Check out these titles to meet more scientists who are out in the field—and contributing every day to our knowledge of the world around us:

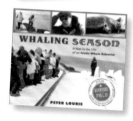

Looking for even more adventure? Craving updates on the work of your favorite scientists, as well as in-depth video footage, audio, photography, and more? Then visit the Scientists in the Field website!

www.sciencemeetsadventure.com